Remains of the Journey

Souvenirs of the Real and Imagined

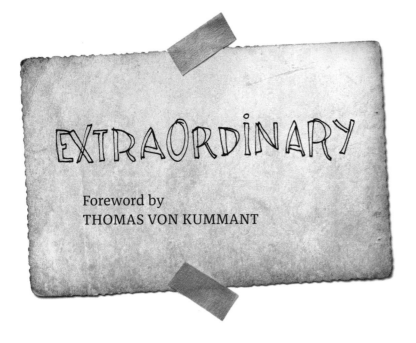

EXTRAORDINARY

Foreword by
THOMAS VON KUMMANT

Who doesn't love zapping through the world of new art, ever-present in these days of *Artstation, Instagram, Twitter* and *Facebook*? The internet is full of it and the sheer quantity is immense.

You can find concept and storyboard artists, character designers, matte painters, illustrators, 3D artists, comic artists, contemporary painters, motion graphics, architecture, installations, product design, virtual reality, the list goes on and on – it's fantastic! The flood of images gushes by before your eyes and the attention span soon dwindles to lower levels. From time to time, though, an artist stands head and shoulders above the crowd and grabs my attention. This preface is dedicated to one of these.

How would I describe Jörg Asselborn's illustrations?
Vibrantly lively, wonderfully weird and refreshingly quirky!

I draw every day to earn my living – and my illustrations visualise ideas and stories. Now, you might think that illustrators are more than happy to put their pencil down for a while when they have some spare time – take a break, do some back exercises, that sort of thing. That's not how it works, though. Every trip and holiday fuels my craving to capture moments, people and places in my sketchpad with my pencil or brush. For me, a moment becomes even more vivid when captured on paper. The first time I noticed this was when I drew my dear grandmother on her deathbed.

It is, then, all the more strange that I didn't discover the *Urban Sketchers* until ten years after they were founded. After all, this is a worldwide community of like-minded people, who mostly work in groups to capture their surroundings, impressions of their travels, or life in their home towns in their drawings. I saw a drawing by Jörg Asselborn on the *Urban Sketchers* Facebook page for the first time towards the end of 2017 – *"Mercedes-Benz LK 388 Tipper from 1960"*. This was drawn in a casual three-point perspective, with extremely loose lines and watercolour pigments left to do whatever they wanted for colouring. "Extraordinary," I thought.

After that, I kept noticing his incredibly vivid illustrations on Facebook. The way Jörg draws and colours things is fascinating in itself, but on top of that, his eye for interesting motifs is unique. His *"L'Observatoire de Cointe Liège"* drawing prompted me to imme-diately dive in and research and select photos of the building.

An almost documentary approach which, in the case of the "Völklinger Hütte" drawings, shows how closely Jörg Asselborn observes, consciously absorbs everything, then reproduces it in his own style.

The Urban Sketchers have been meeting every year since 2010 for their symposium, each time in a different city, attracting artists from all corners of the globe. Selected artists offer workshops. Finally, in 2019, I managed to find the time to register for the Urban Sketchers Symposium in Amsterdam. The city is just wonderful for drawing and – because I would be keen to offer a workshop myself – I was interested in how these things are structured. All workshops were fully booked within 2 hours of sales going online and I was lucky enough to get a place on the "Catching windmills" workshop by Jörg Asselborn, and to experience this in Amsterdam. The spontaneity of his illustrations comes from "blind drawing". You study the object then sketch it without looking down at the page. Details and colours come later and are set loosely on the sheet; the somewhat low viscosity of the colours is a defining feature. I found it fascinating to watch Jörg's demonstration of his technique.

The pictures my daughters and nieces drew and painted when they were young have a similar magical attraction for me. This is a very self-confident way of putting an idea, an experience, a thought, a pattern or a song clearly and boldly onto a blank sheet of paper, then filling it with life. Children also have this untarnished way of creating with a pencil or brush and their spontaneous strokes and overlapping colours create exciting textures and strangely peculiar silhouettes. Jörg Asselborn has a wonderful way of creating quirky illustrations; ones where you can literally see the ease with which they were created. Whether they are objects, architecture, vehicles, figures or landscapes, his illustrations have the same magical attraction to me and I can recognise Jörg Asselborn's work at first glance.

His method and spontaneous strokes slightly distort the proportions and shapes. Nevertheless, you're still left with the feeling that the machine, building, car, or windmill would still work perfectly anyway. Every detail is immaculately researched, it all has its place and is part of a whole. Function and form fit seamlessly together, resulting in a new lively, quirky and extraordinary structure within the Asselborn universe.

I would love to see a classic animated film in Jörg Asselborn's style and I enjoy musing over what kind of story could possibly do justice to these drawings. What would be the music to reflect the mood of his wonderful designs and what characters would fill this quirky world? Perhaps you might have your own thoughts while leafing through the following pages?

I am so looking forward to the post-corona period, to the next Urban Sketchers Symposium and every new drawing that comes out of this unique and wonderful artist.

Dachau, May 2020.

BUILDINGS AND PLACES

In 2010, during a period when I was drawing very little, I tuned in to a radio programme about the Berlin Urban Sketchers (the Urban Sketchers are an international community of illustrators. They meet up to draw their urban environment and then share the images they create on location with the online world*. These drawings are often "immortalised" in sketchbooks).

Of course, using a sketchbook and drawing on location was nothing new to me. But after my studies, I simply wasn't managing to take sketchbooks with me regularly on my solo trips or excursions, let alone filling one. So even before I had finished listening to the radio show about them, I knew that this is what I had to do: go out and draw together with other artists on location.

CHAPELLE DU
SAINT SÉPULCRE

PEYROLLES-EN-PROV.

* To find out more, visit: *www.urbansketchers.org*

I very often draw buildings because the cityscape usually provides the stage for the motifs I prefer. People, on the other hand, move too fast for my kind of illustrations so they don't often appear in my sketches. Buildings do not move – so I have all the time I need to draw them.

Older houses and buildings in particular bear fascinating witness: not only of the times they have lived through, but also of their inhabitants. The distinctive lines of their ageing tell me stories, which I try to convey in my drawings. They give every house and building its own special personality that I strive to capture.

LIÈGE

RUE DU PARLEMENT

BERUMER MÜHLE
23.XII.15

LIMBURG
BLICK VOM DOMBERG
ZUM NONNENGRABEN

DIÖZESANMUSEUM
LIMBURG

20
11
16

FISCHMARKT
LIMBURG

HESSENPARK

NEBENGEBAÜDE
AUS FRANKENBACH

ERBAUT 1848

st. Michae
Mount
(castle.)

16
10
13

St Ives. 18
Smeaton's 10
Pier 13

13

BOULVD.
ALFRED GUILLOU,
CONCARNEAU

BLD. ALFRED GUILLOU
CONCARNEAU

HAMBURG, DEICHTOR- HALLEN

KEHRWIEDER SPITZE
(HAFENPOLIZEIWACHE № 2)

SHOREDITCH HIGH STREET LONDON

ST. CHADS
HAGGERSTON,
LONDON

15
08
17

FROM
FOTO

21

HOTEL

LIÈGE
CHAUSSÉE
DES PRÉS

L'OBSERVATOIRE DE COINTE LIÈGE

23

LIÈGE - RUE SAINTE-CATHERINE

RUA NOVA DA ALFANDEGA, PORTO

PORTO, RUA DE CIMA DO MURO

HOLZKIRCHEN

IGREJA PAROQUIAL
DE SÃO NICOLAU

KLOSTER LORSCH
"KÖNIGSHALLE"

WALKMÜHLE
WIESBADEN

WALKMÜHLE
WIESBADEN
10
04
16

WIESBADEN,
SCHLACHTHOF,
KESSELHAUS

CE LIEU FUT LE DERNIÈR SÉJOUR
APRÈS TANT DE SUFFRANCE
D'HOMMES ENTRAÎNÉS
PAR LA GUERRE VERS LEUR
TRAGIQUE DESTIN
MAISON D'ARRÊT DE
PONTANIOU
AOÛT 1944

BREST, RUE DE PONTANIOU

St FERRÉO
LES COMB

29
08
1A

PFARRHAUS
der RUSSISCH-
ORTHODOXEN
KIRCHE

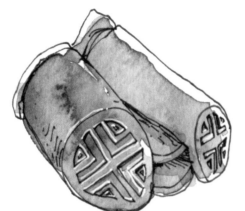

GRÜNEBURG-PARK
KOREANISCHER GARTEN
FRANKFURT A.M.

GREYMOUTH, NEXT TO THE TRAIN STATION (NZ)

FLEET-
SCHLÖSSCHEN,
HAMBURG
SPEICHERSTADT

JONAS DANIEL
MEIJERPLEIN

~ CENTRUM ~

AMSTERDAM

1897

DE GOOYER

FUNENKADE,
AMSTERDAM

KOOG AAN DE ZAAN

JULIUS BOESEL HOUSE

SPECIAL PLACES: VÖLKLINGER HÜTTE – VÖLKLINGEN IRONWORKS

The Völklinger Hütte is an ironworks in Völklingen in Saarland, near the border with the French Lorraine region. After a lifetime of more than 100 years, part of the plant, the "pig-iron phase", was closed down in 1986 and placed under the protection of historic buildings and monuments. The ironworks became an industrial monument. UNESCO declared this part of the Völklinger Hütte a "World Cultural Heritage Site" in 1994.

It is fantastic to draw here – but at the same time, it's a challenge to seek out the right motifs. Everything is so overwhelming – gigantic and intertwined. The functions of the countless conveyor belts, machines, pipes and cables are not immediately apparent. I like to concentrate on those details and individual elements that I can understand: a boiler in front of a house, a locomotive, a chunky control panel or the striking shapes of ascending pipes and their vents. The atmosphere in this overpowering moloch of a building is fascinating,

everything is covered with rust. Decay is everywhere. And yet at the same time, everything looks just as if the workers left their shift at the factory a mere few hours ago. In actual fact, everything did remain untouched after its closure.

This meant I was able to draw a locker complete with tools, screws, oil cans and other work paraphernalia that had been standing there all this time. I also drew a 'break-time bench' in the sintering hall. I read that in this hall, residual materials such as fine ore and blast furnace dust from the smelting process were recycled so that they could be reused in the blast furnaces. The gigantic shredders made an unbelievable noise with dirt and ashes incessantly raining down from above. The workers in the sintering hall had to take their meal breaks right there as no break rooms or similar facilities were provided for them. So, those workers from the 1960s built a make-shift shelter entirely from waste material – wooden planks, boards, roofing felt and felt mats – to protect themselves from the dust and particles raining down onto them while they were eating.

I find that kind of thing very impressive. There are no people in my drawings, but I do visualise them in all the objects from the past that I draw. I try to imagine how long I would last under these working conditions. Not very long, I am quite sure of that.

BEI DER
KOKSBATTERIE 7

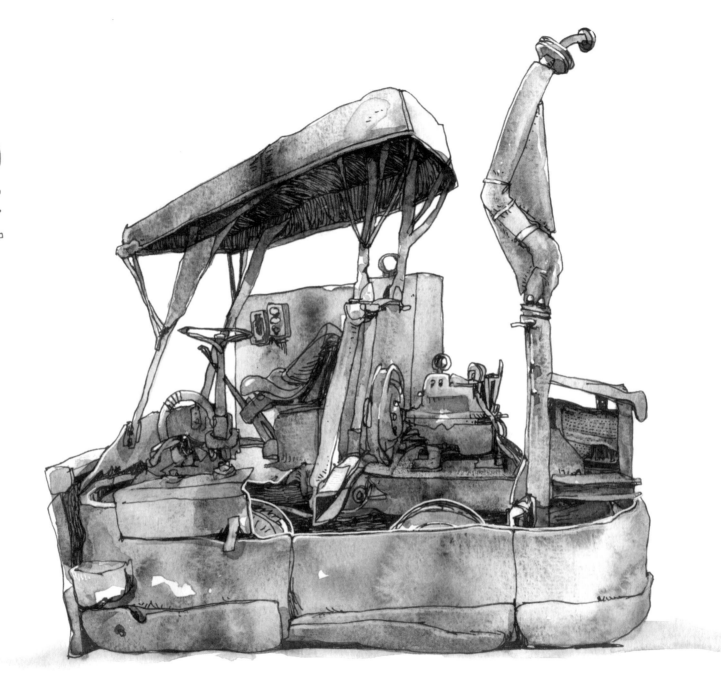

FAHRZEUG ZUM KOKSSCHIEBEN
VÖLKLINGER HÜTTE, KOKEREI

ÖLKANNEN
AUS
WERKZEUG-
SPIND

PAUSENBANK

IN DER SINTERANLAGE.
ETWA IN DEN 1960ER JAHREN
ENTSTANDEN.
UM SICH VOR DEM STAUB DER
ANLAGE ZU SCHÜTZEN, ZIMMERTEN
SICH DIE ARBEITER DIESEN
UNTERSTAND MIT EINER BANK.

VÖLKLINGER HÜTTE
30. SEPTEMBER '17

ARBEITERSPIND
ZUSTAND BEI ÖFFNUNG 1998

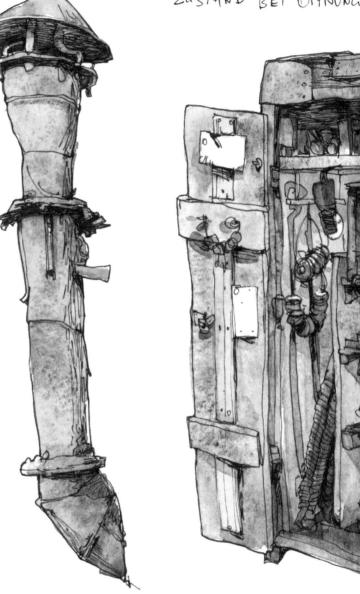

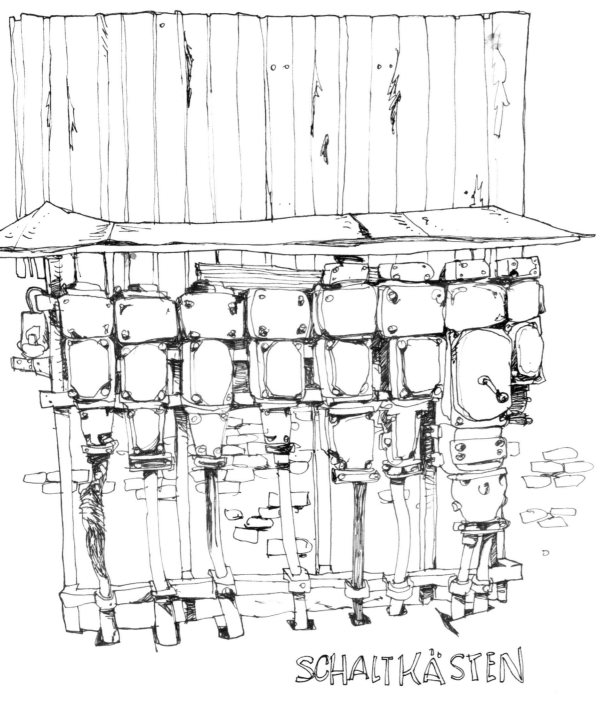

SCHALTKÄSTEN

HOLZ-SPIND

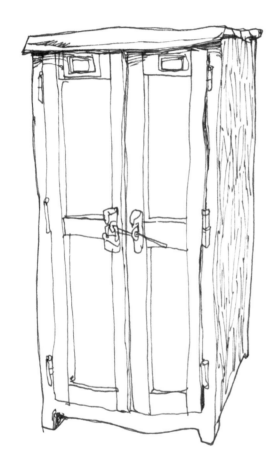

KOHLEZUG

JUNG

BAUJAHR 1964

BLICK VON DER
ERZHALLE

VÖLKLINGER HÜTTE:
RÜCKSEITE DER HANDWERKER-
GASSE

SPECIAL PLACES: ÎLE D'OUESSANT (USHANT)

In May 2019, I spent a few days on this island, 20 km off the coast of Brittany at the edge of the Celtic Sea. Ouessant, or Ushant as it is known in English, is the westernmost part of France. Together with a group of wonderful and highly-regarded illustrators, I spent three days in exceptionally calm and beautiful weather drawing the "cabinet of curiosities" that is l'île d'Ouessant: dramatic shipwreck remnants in the Musée des Phares, buoys, boats, car wrecks at the island's official scrapyard, trees bent by the wind and the prehistoric stone circle of Pen-ar-Lan on the edge of the cliffs, high above the sea.

COMMISSION DES PHARES EN 1863.

LA CASSE, PORT DU STIFF ÎLE D'OUESSANT

LE CROMLECH
POINTE DE PENN ARLAN
ÎLE D'OUESSANT

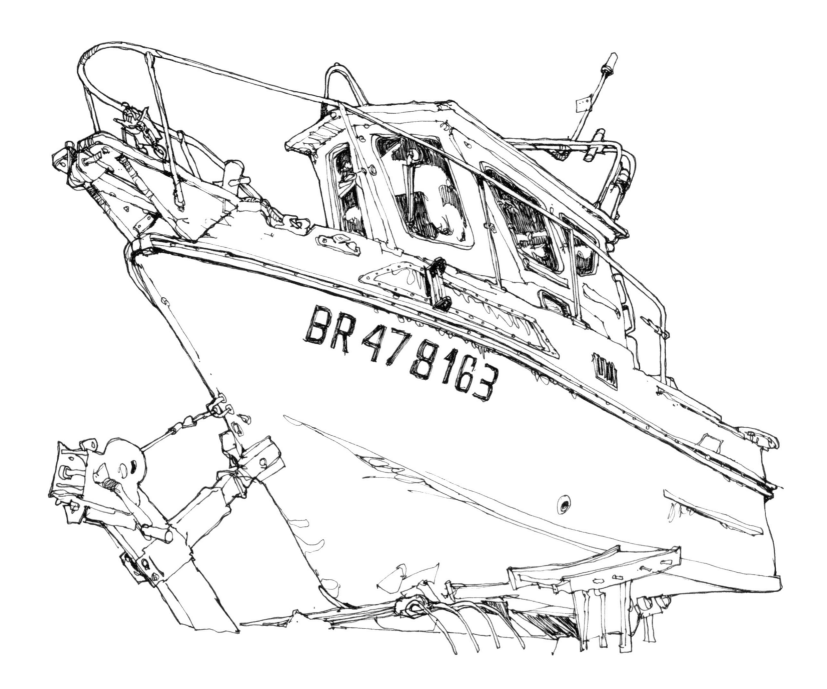

TRIBORD

BABORD

CLOCHE SOUS-MARINE

P C

ÉLÉMENTS DE RÉAS
PROVENANT DE
L'ÉPAVE DU Séduisant
1796

ÎLE D'OUESSANT , LE STIFF

58

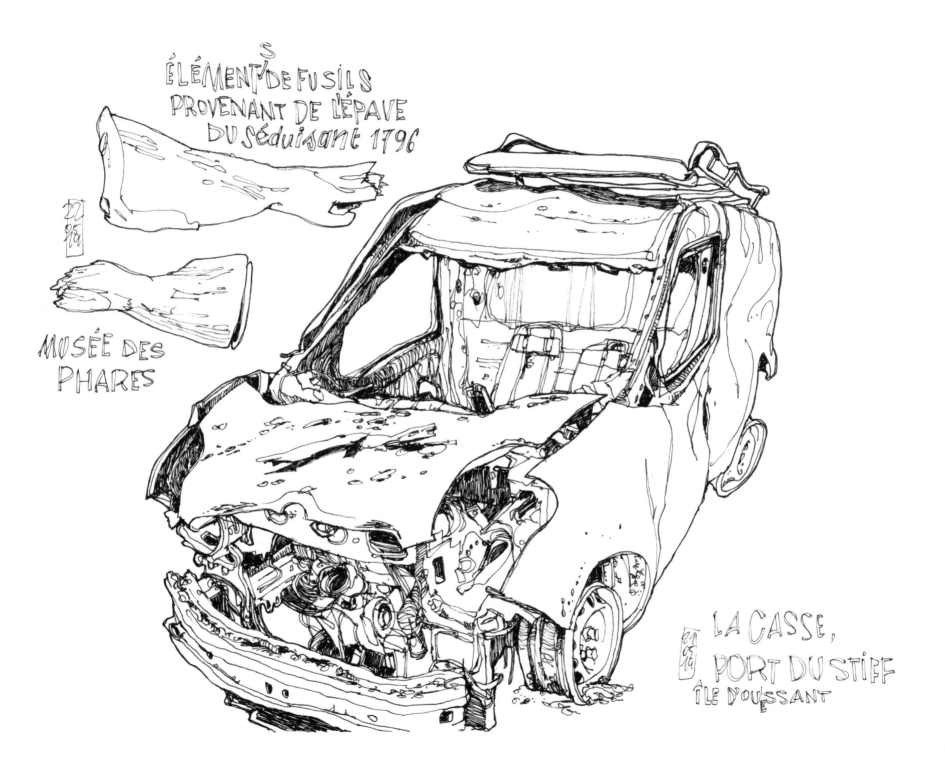

ÉLÉMENTS DE FUSILS
PROVENANT DE L'ÉPAVE
DU SÉDUISANT 1796

MUSÉE DES
PHARES

LA CASSE,
PORT DU STIFF
ÎLE D'OUESSANT

PLACES THAT DON'T EXIST

Most of my drawings were created on location, on journeys or excursions, the motifs discovered either by chance or at an intended destination. Every now and then I discover places on the Internet which I probably won't be able to visit any time soon, or perhaps even at all, but which inspire me to draw them just by looking at them. Some of the following drawings are a blend of reality and fiction: images from the World Wide Web mixed with my memories of travelling to other places. If any such places existed, they would be at the top of my travel wish-list.

THE LOVEGOOD HOUSE

"THE BURROW"
WARNER BROTHERS STUDIOS,
LONDON

65

VEHICLES, BOATS AND AIRCRAFT

Even as a child, I drew cars a lot. Mostly Opel models, which I often "painted" as a side view. Car, plane and ship quartet games were an integral part of every child's birthday goodie-bag and were a great pastime, on long car journeys, for example (in a life before smartphones). I could build metre-long traffic jams out of my *Majorette* or *Matchbox* cars and still have some left over. Looking back, you could say that car industry marketing has worked brilliantly.

Having said that, cars are today, and have always been, the design objects of their time, visible everywhere and every day. Their design language emanates from a special epoch yet expresses the state of the art and aesthetic taste of their time.

When I draw a car, I think of the films, TV series or comics where this model features, or of the people or events I associate with the car.

I find it particularly nice when I'm not the only one doing that: once, for instance, when I was drawing a small Messerschmitt Kabinenroller cabin scooter (a German miniature car from the post-war and "economic miracle" years) in a museum, an older lady spoke to me. She reminisced about weekend family outings for three (which is remarkable in itself given the lack of space inside!) in the 1950s and had tears in her eyes when she finally resumed her tour.

What fascinates me about boats is the variety of shapes – almost no two boats are alike, each one seeming to have been built to very specific ideas and for very specific functions. I especially like to draw small boats, wooden fishing boats, barges, steel fishing cutters or sailing boats, where you can see their age and the fact that they have been in use over a long time. I have a similar passion for drawing aeroplanes, or should I say flying machines: the more distinctive they are, the more interesting they seem to me. I finish off the surface textures and shapes during the colouration phase.

OPEL OLYMPIA

70

MINERVA 1916
ORIGINALSTATE FROM WWI

MERCEDES-BENZ
LK 388 KIPPER (1960)

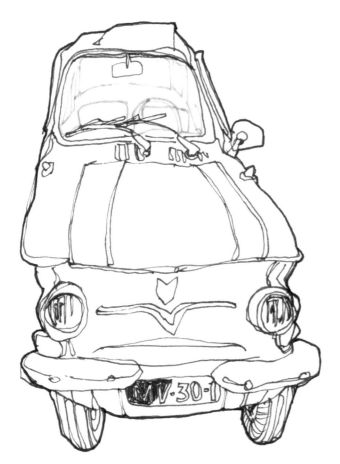

1963

NSU
PRINZ 4

NSU
RO 80
1973

OPEL DIPLOMAT
B V8
1973

Museum Speyer

Méhari

ST-BONNET-DU-GARD

878 XX 30

PONTIAC
» GRAND VILLE «

MUSEO AUTOMOUILÍSTICA
MÁLAGA
PANHARD
ET LEVASSOR
1938

"THE NOON
DEVIL"

MAPUA
LEISURE
PARK,
MAPUA, NZ

KNIGHT BUS

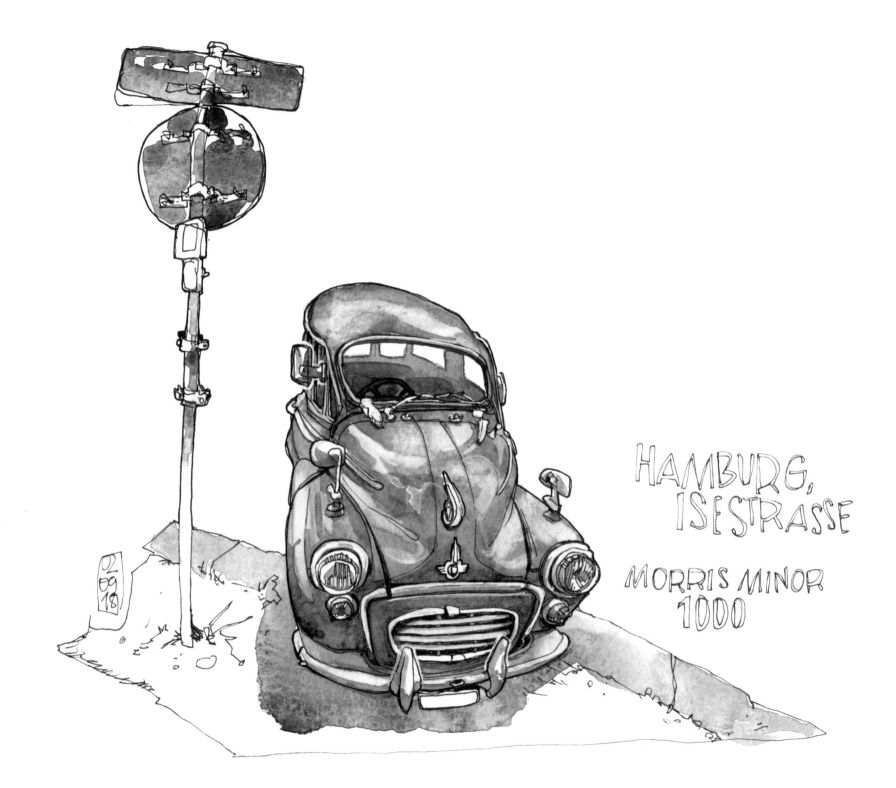

HAMBURG,
ISESTRASSE

MORRIS MINOR
1000

FORD ANGLIA
105E DELUXE

7990 TD

FORD 130
TRANSIT

WI·LW2H

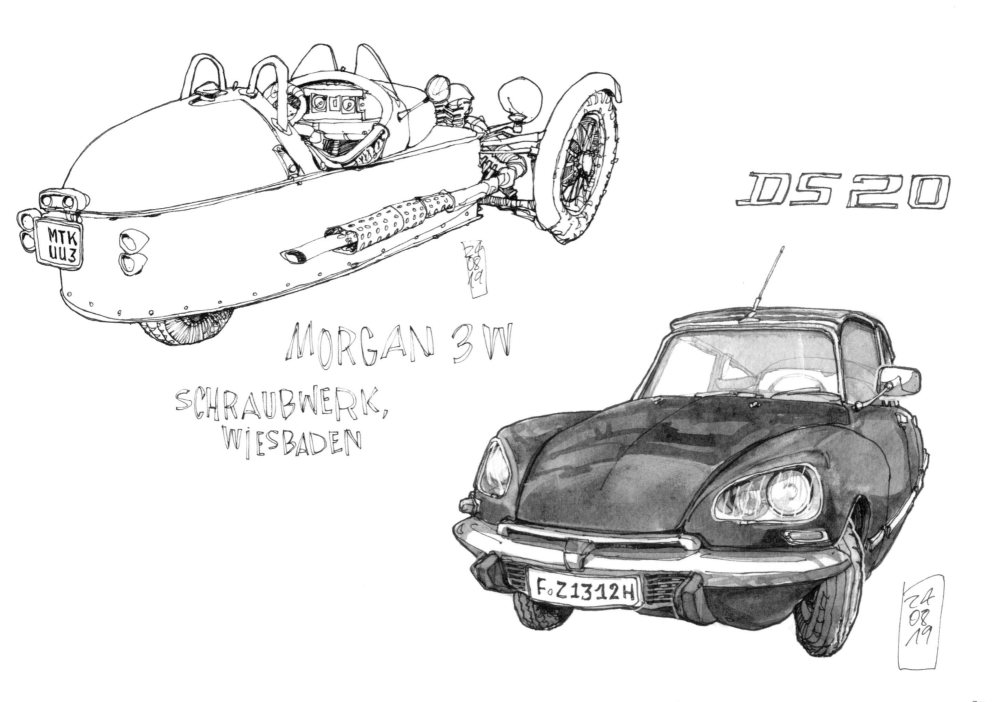

MORGAN 3W

SCHRAUBWERK,
WIESBADEN

DS 20

MTK
UU3

F·Z1312H

VOLVO
ECR145D L

WALKMÜHLE
WIESBADEN

NASSAUKADE
AMSTERDAM

KLEINWAGEN

14
09
19
NR 12-4973

EISENBAHN MUSEUM
DARMSTADT KRANICHSTEIN

MUSÉE DES
ARTS ET MÉTIERS,
PARIS

»AVION 3«

AVION 3/AÉROPLANE DE CLÉMENT ADER / 1893 – 1897

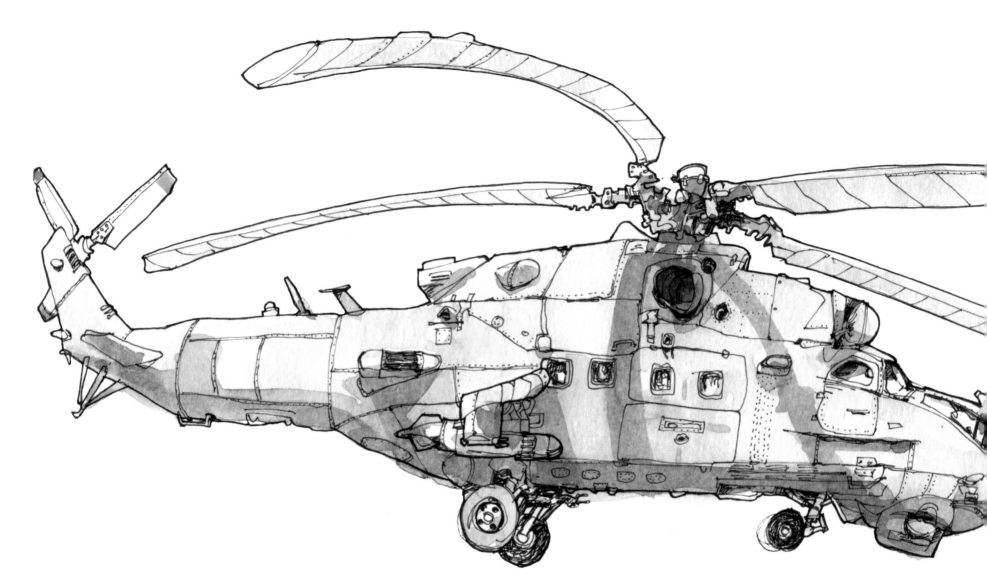

MIL MI 24 P

PANHARD
& LEVASSEUR

CAPRONI
CA 22

CAPRONI - 1913

OMAKA AVIATION
HERITAGE CENTRE,
BLENHEIM (NZ)

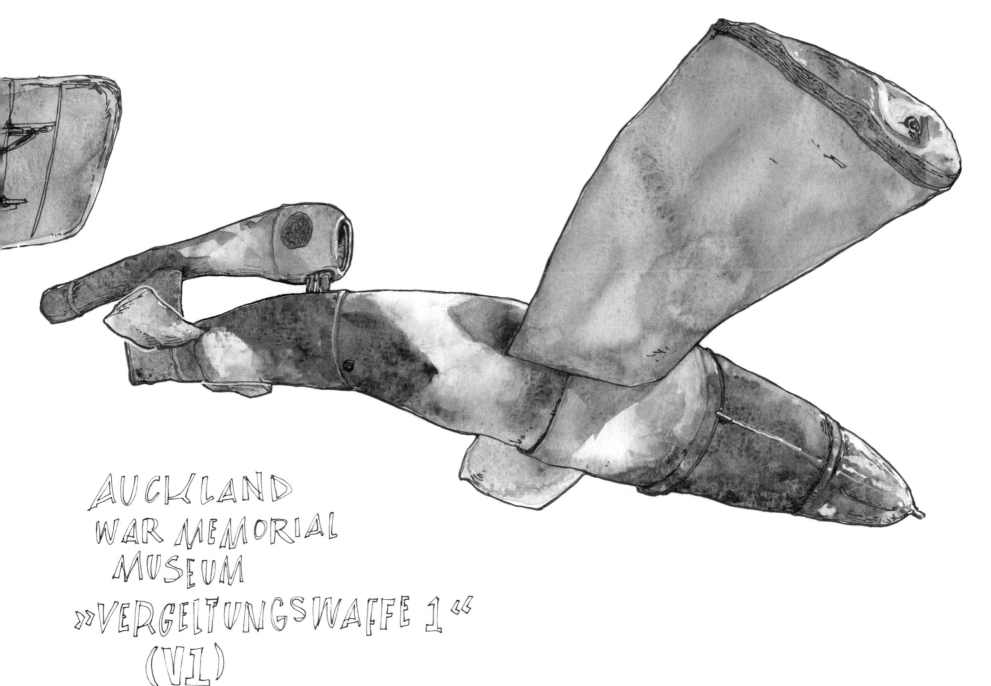

AUCKLAND
WAR MEMORIAL
MUSEUM
»VERGELTUNGSWAFFE 1«
(V1)

ROEI-
JACHTJE

26
07
11

ANSTEUERUNGS-
TONNE

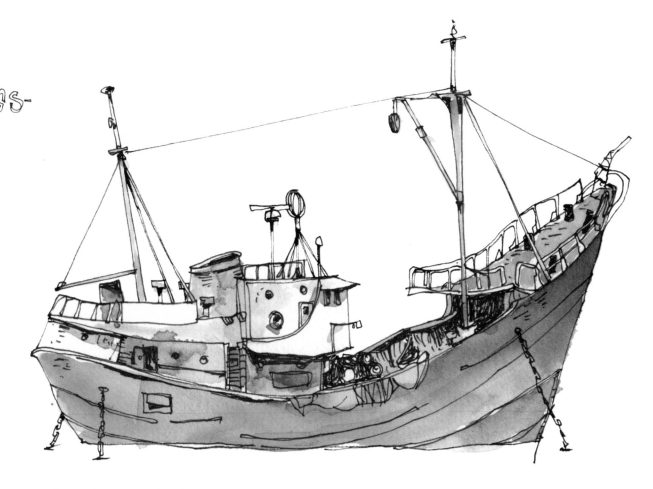

HEMERICA,
CONCARNEAU

CONCARNEAU,
HAFEN 20.07.16

KLEINST UNTERSEEBOOT
»SEEHUND«

2700

Athena Fay

PZ49

Z49

+5 min.

18 St. Ives
10 Smeaton's
13 Pier

Flood!

BOTE DEL PRÁCTICO
MÁLAGA PUERTO

5-MA4-2-95

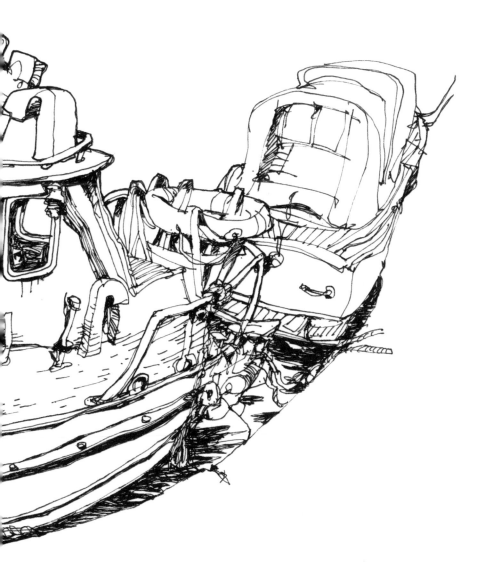

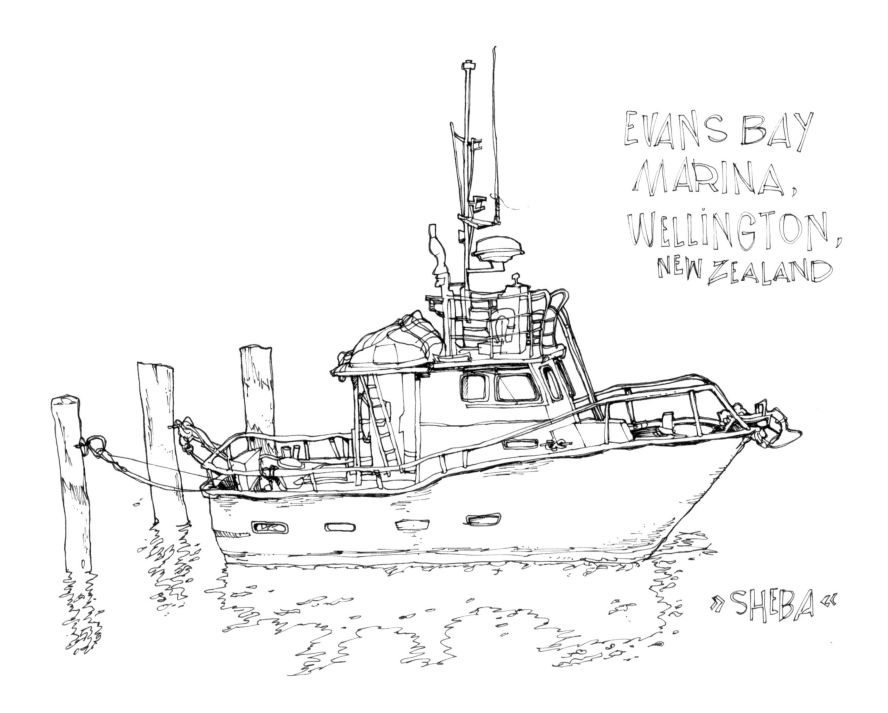

EVANS BAY
MARINA,
WELLINGTON,
NEW ZEALAND

»SHEBA«

"MAGELLAN"

CAMARET-
SUR-MER
17
05 (FROM
17 PHOTO)

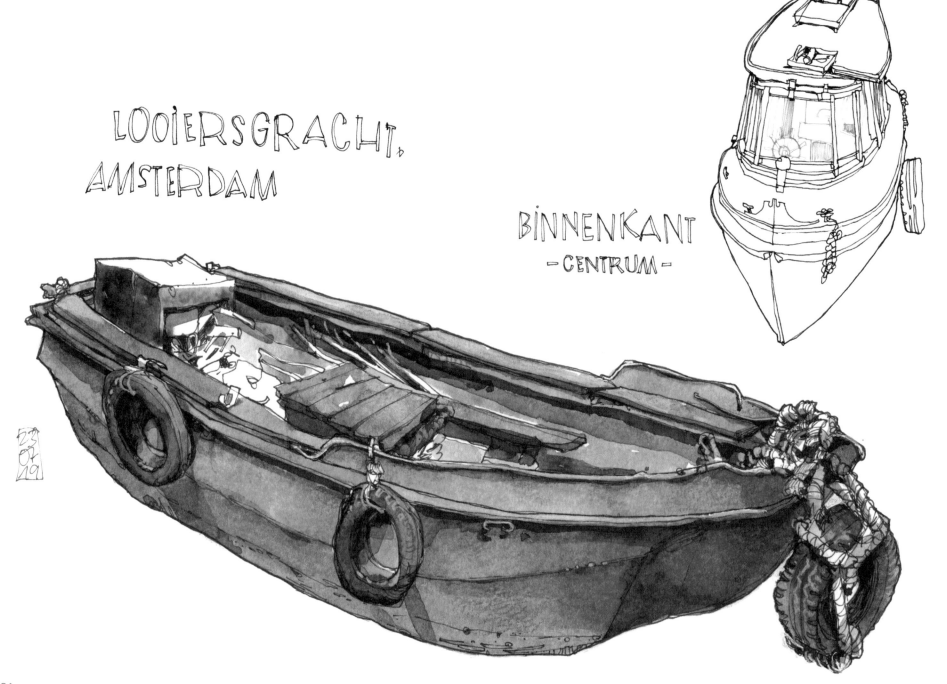

LOOIERSGRACHT,
AMSTERDAM

BINNENKANT
- CENTRUM -

CONCARNEAU PORT 26 07 16

CABINET OF CURIOSITIES

The 'cabinets of curiosities' coveted by the aristocracy or the rich bourgeoisie in the late Renaissance and Baroque periods were the forerunners of the museums of today. They were used to show off curiosities of differing origins and types, irrespective of whether they bore any relation to each other in terms of content or not.

Similarly, I like to draw objects that do not necessarily have any "common thread" – things I discover by chance – exhibits from museums (especially in winter when it's too cold to draw outdoors), or things I just happen to notice in passing. If these are metallic or wooden objects, they tend to deform and change over time. They weather, they rust, they warp or are sometimes badly damaged. They provide a plethora of interesting shapes and textures for drawing and wonderful surfaces whose textures and colours are so well suited for watercolour painting...

Sometimes you glean clues and hear stories about their origins, about people who made or owned these things, or the functions these things once played. Especially, of course, when you are drawing in a museum. With a little bit of imagination, though, you can make up a wonderful story yourself.

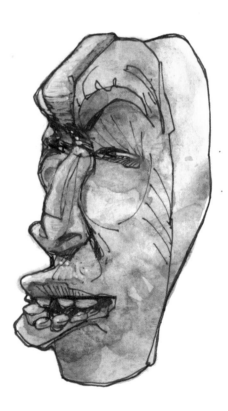

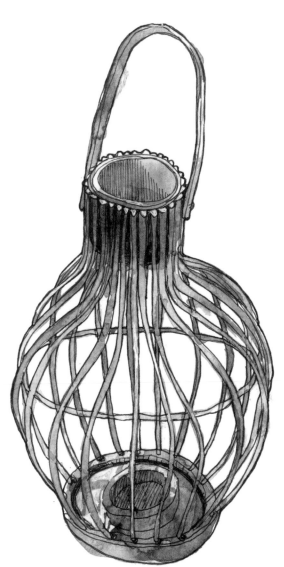

LATERNE

SENCKEN-
BERG MUSEUM
FRANKFURT

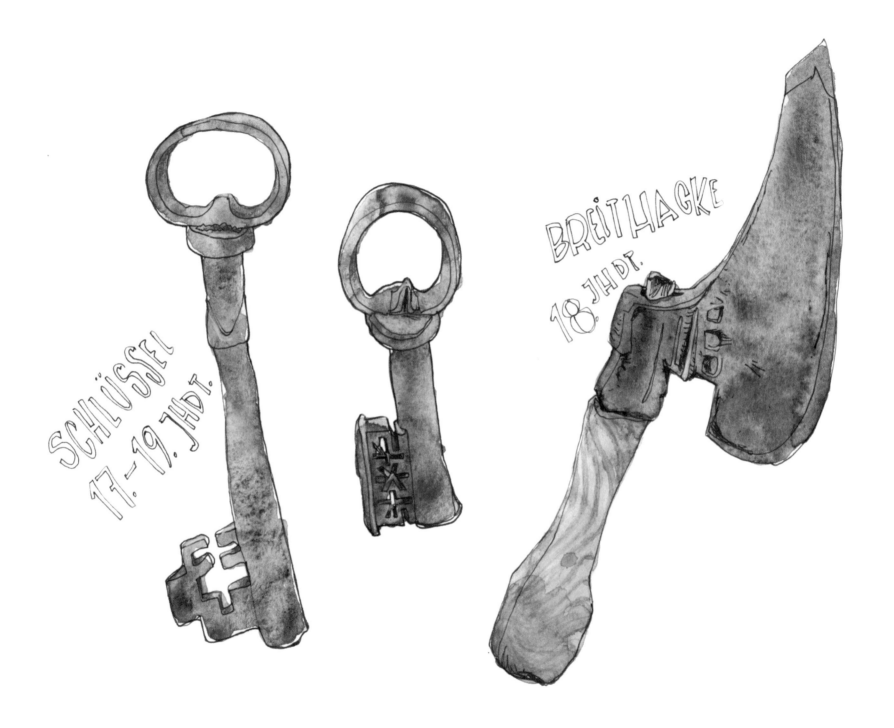

SCHLÜSSEL
17.-19. JHDT.

BREITHACKE
18. JHDT.

27
12
18

AUCKLAND
WAR MEMORIAL
MUSEUM

111

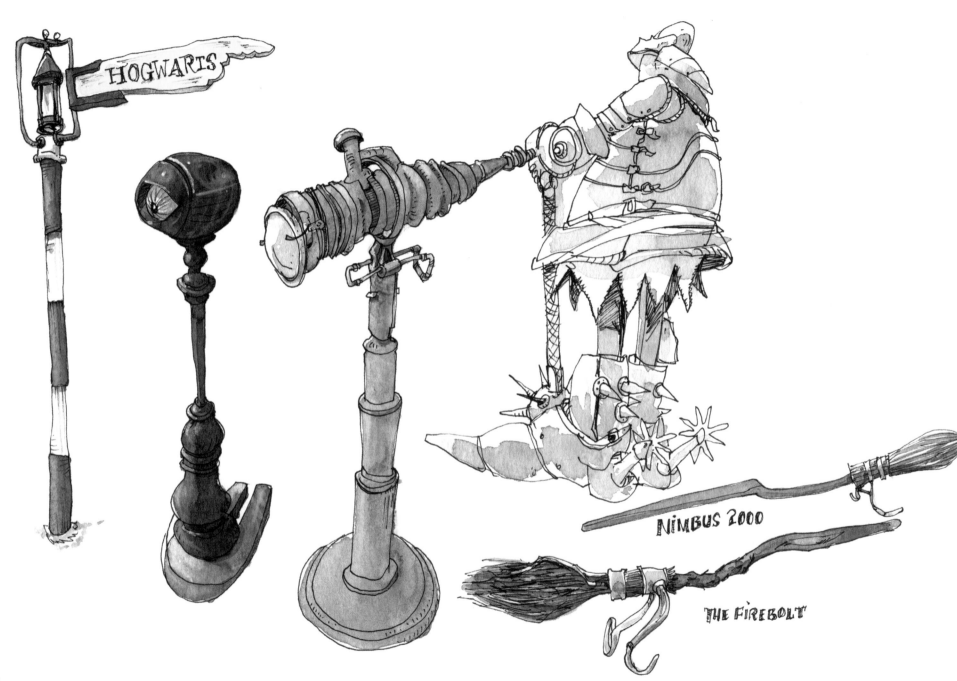

HOGWARTS

NIMBUS 2000

THE FIREBOLT

HARRYS
HAMBURGER
HAFENBASAR

HARRY

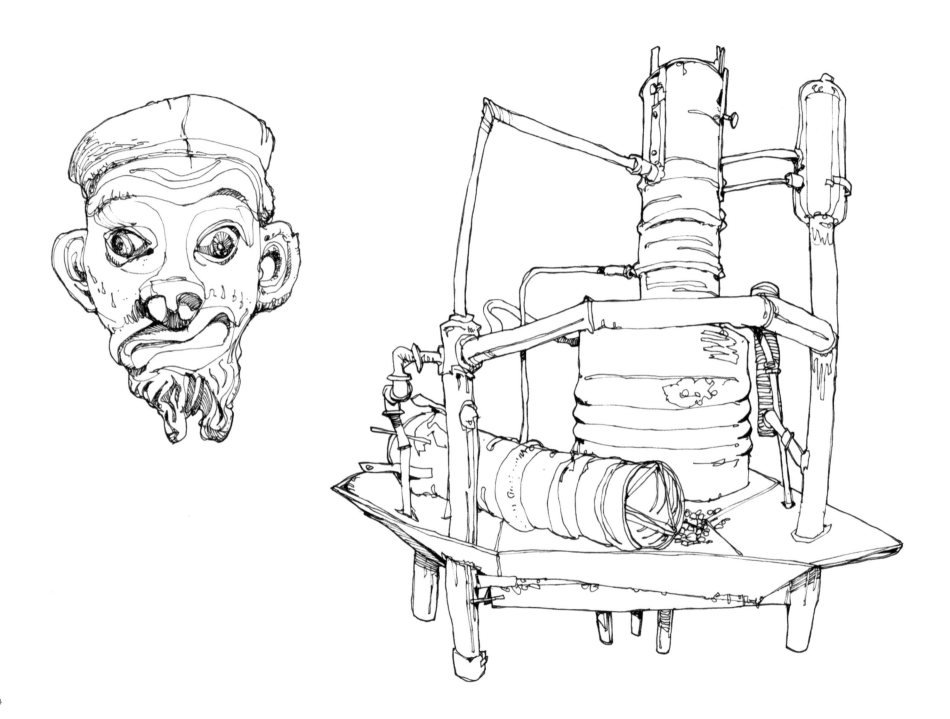

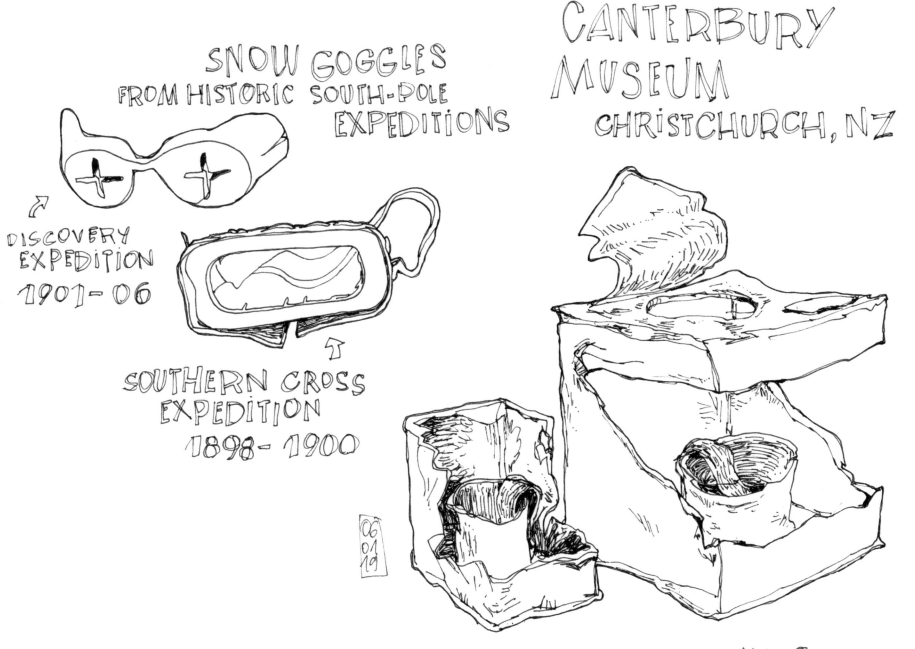

SNOW GOGGLES
FROM HISTORIC SOUTH-POLE
EXPEDITIONS

CANTERBURY
MUSEUM
CHRISTCHURCH, NZ

DISCOVERY
EXPEDITION
1901-06

SOUTHERN CROSS
EXPEDITION
1898-1900

IMPROVISED BLUBBER LAMPS

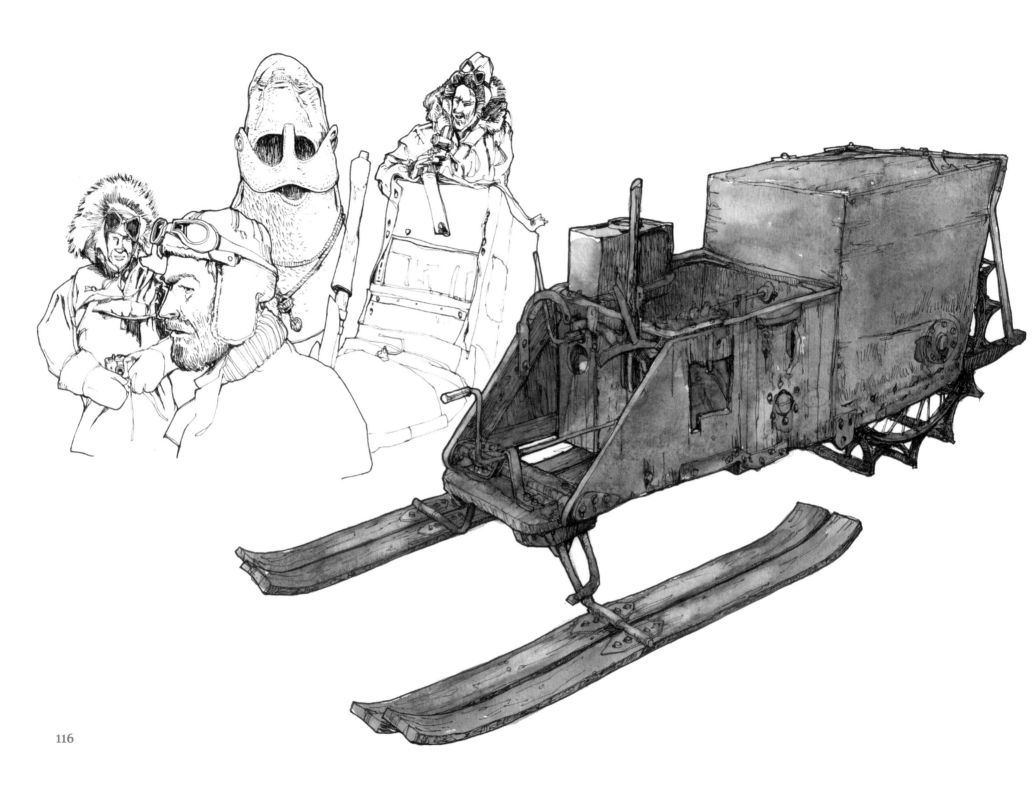

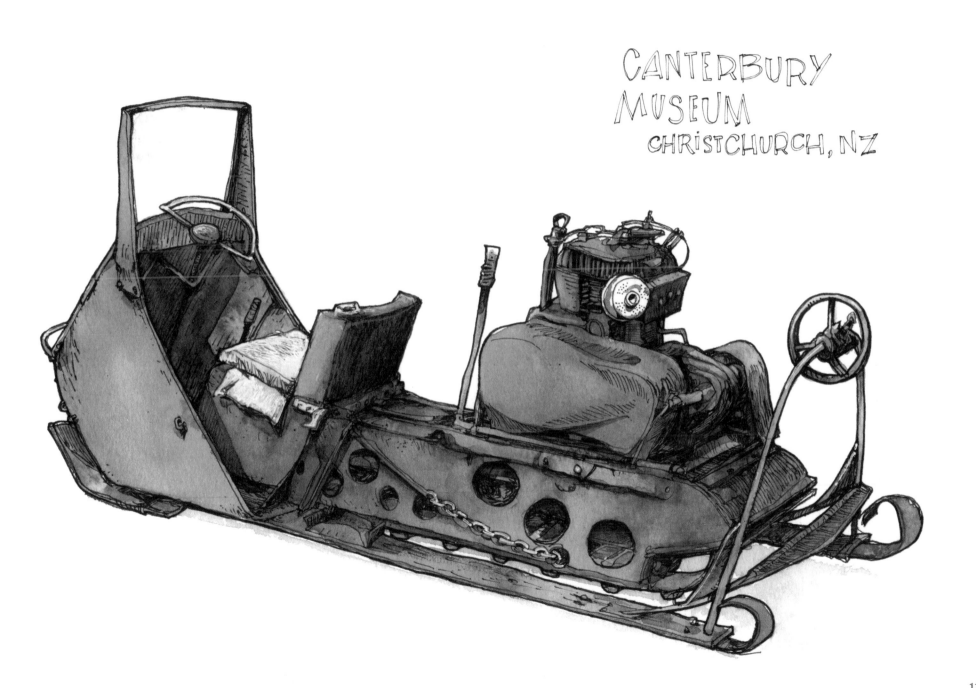

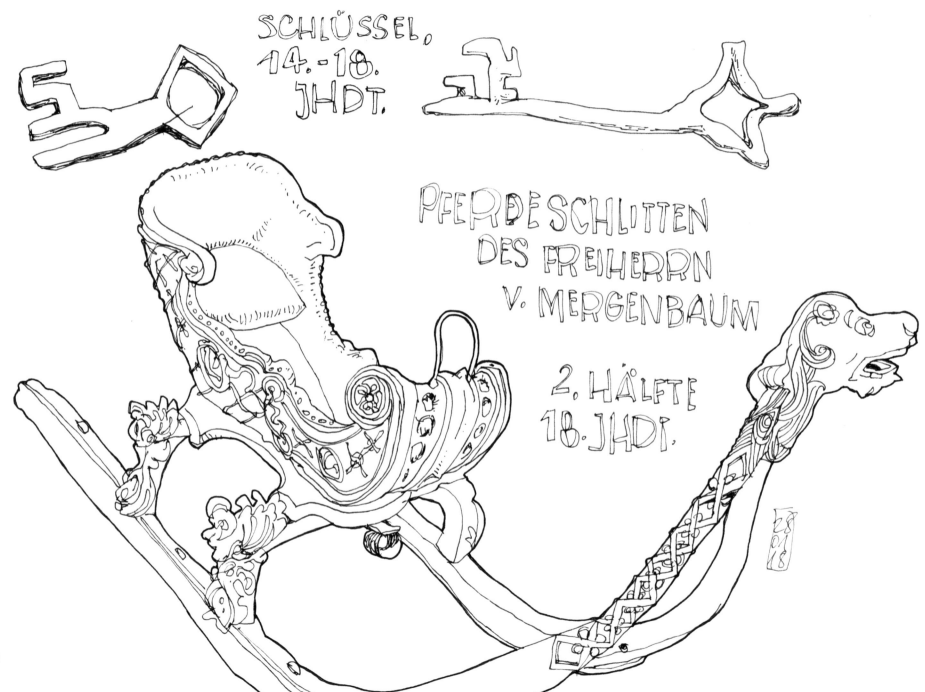

SCHLÜSSEL,
14.-18.
JHDT.

PFERDESCHLITTEN
DES FREIHERRN
V. MERGENBAUM

2. HÄLFTE
18. JHDT.

TEMPEL DES
HERCULES VICTOR

KORKMODELL VON
CARL MAY

IM SCHLOSS JOHANNIS-
BURG, ASCHAFFENBURG
MASSSTAB CA. 1:50

28
01
18

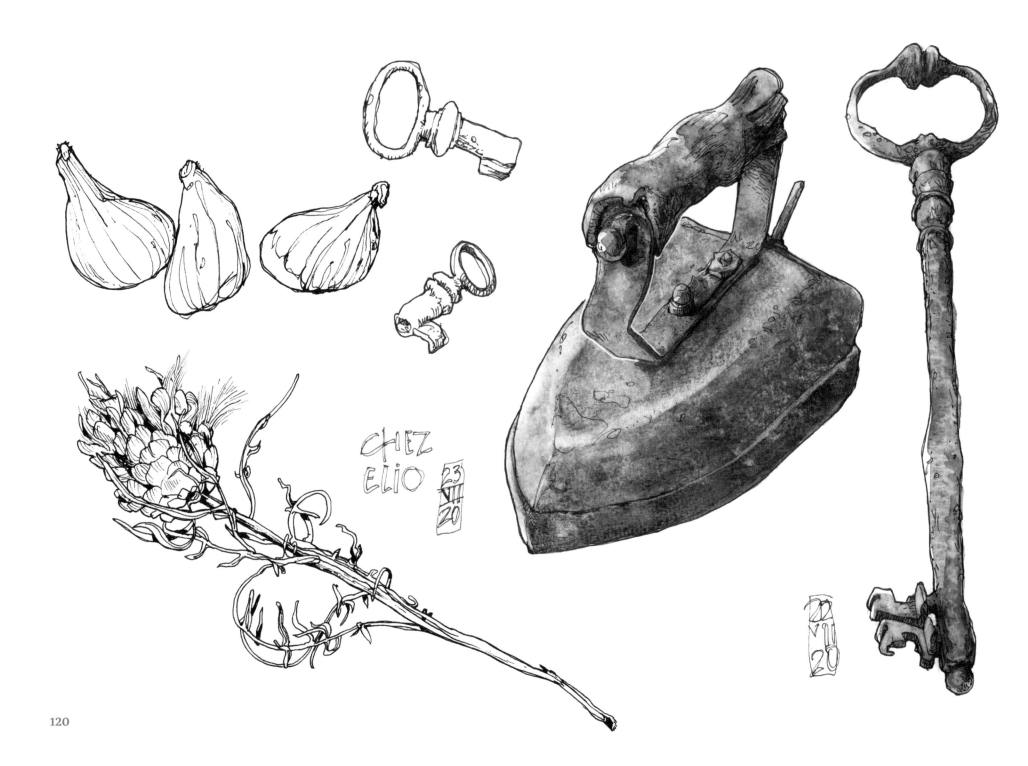

CHEZ
ELIO

HESSENPARK

CITADELLE
DE FORCALQUIER
(STUDY FROM FOTO)

TREES

I love drawing trees. Special trees – particularly old ones or trees with unusually shaped trunks. Actually, I mostly draw the trunk and branches, hardly ever the crown and leaves. I like to lose myself in all its twists and turns, the overlapping of branches and twigs, but still try to capture the "grand design" of the tree, its bearing, its angle.

There are definitely rules with trees that should be observed, but unlike architecture, there are no straight lines (which I don't pay attention to anyway) and there is no axial symmetry whatsoever.

Over the past few years, trees have become something like a "Plan B" for me. When I feel that I'm a little too tense when I am drawing, or when I have too little patience to deal with parallels and converging lines, I look for a tree as a motif. Trees make you happy.

ALONG THE WAY TO
CATHEDRAL COVE
COROMANDEL, NZ

« JE SUIS NÉ
EN L'AN 908 »

PONT
DU GARD

IN GELHEIM

125

PEYROLLES-
EN-PROVENCE

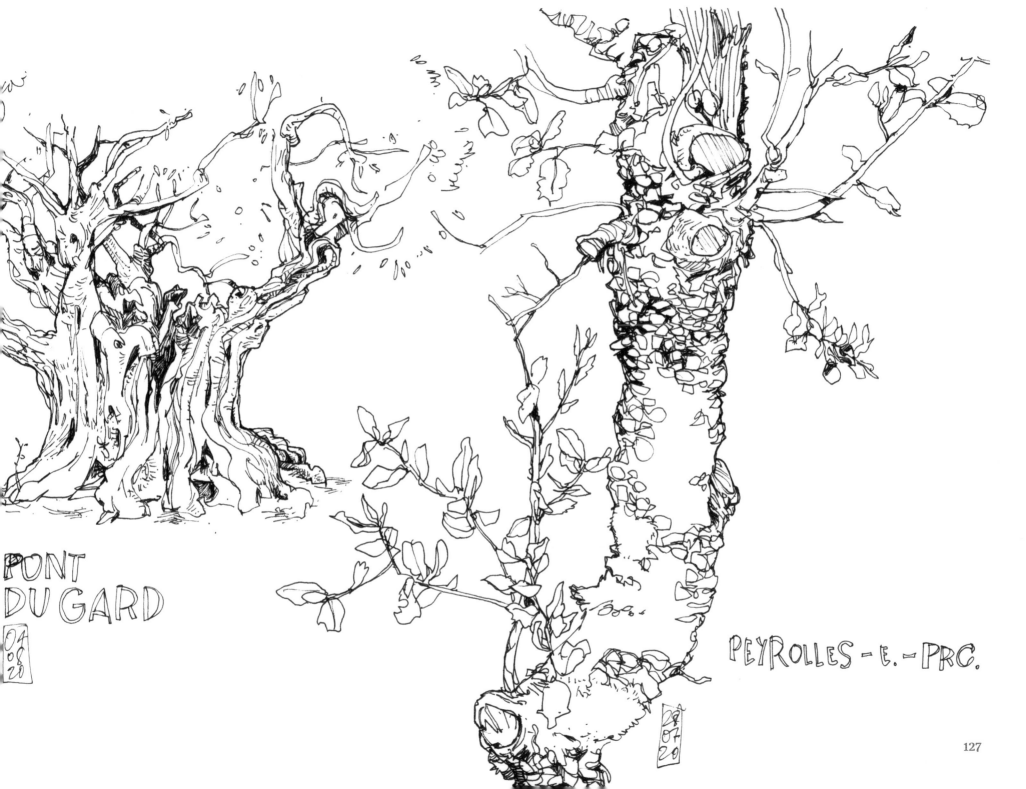

PONT
DU GARD

PEYROLLES - E. - PRC.

127

PONT DU GARD, FRANCE

REMAINS OF THE JOURNEY

EDITIONS
CAURETTE

© 2021 Éditions Caurette

4 route de Hatten | 67 470 BUHL | France

Rejoignez-nous sur / Come and join us on the web:

[f] editionscaurette   [O] caurette_editions   (globe) www.caurette.com

ISBN 979-10-96315-98-7

Conception graphique / Graphic design: Jörg Asselborn.

Traduction / Translation: Dominica Campman | metatexxt Ltd.

Préface / Foreword: Thomas von Kummant.

Printed in Europe.

Première édition / First Edition

1 000 exemplaires / 1 000 copies